MW01712446

RAISED BED GARDENING FOR BEGINNERS:

A Beginners Guide to Create a Thriving Organic Vegetable Garden with Less Space
(Vegetable Gardening Book 5)

William Urban Green

© Copyright 2020 - all rights reserved.

The content contained within this book may not be reproduced, duplicated or transmitted without direct written permission from the author or the publisher. Under no circumstances will any blame or legal responsibility be held against the publisher, or author, for any damages, reparation, or monetary loss due to the information contained within this book. Either directly or indirectly.

Legal notice: This book is copyright protected. This book is only for personal use. You cannot amend, distribute, sell, use, quote or paraphrase any part, or the content within this book, without the consent of the author or publisher.

Disclaimer notice: Please note the information contained within this document is for educational and entertainment purposes only. All effort has been executed to present accurate, up to date, and reliable, complete information. No warranties of any kind are declared or implied. Readers acknowledge that the author is not engaging in the rendering of legal, financial, medical or professional advice. The content within this book has been derived from various sources. Please consult a licensed professional before attempting any techniques outlined in this book.

By reading this document, the reader agrees that under no circumstances is the author responsible for any losses, direct or indirect, which are incurred as a result of the use of information contained within this document, including, but not limited to, — errors, omissions, or inaccuracies.

Table Of Contents

Introduction

Traditional gardeners have been making use of raised beds to grow their vegetables for many years. They would double dig the beds, creating circular or rectangular mounds a foot or so high with the sloping edges on the sides of the beds. This is especially effective in areas that receive lots of rain since it guarantees good drainage. Additionally, it allows a bit more space to grow your veggies.

Companion planting works perfectly on raised beds. Those vegetables which need more space for their roots like carrots would be planted on top while others like leeks and onions would fill up the space on the sides of your beds. The latter repel pests and would act as a shield for the carrot plants on the top of the bed.

They have added a twist though, now solid frames replace these sloping sides to give the raised beds a distinct and well-defined structure. What this means is that you can make the beds as high or tall as you want them to be without the danger of soil runoff when it rains.

It might sound like a tremendous job, but these modern raised gardening beds are easy to assemble or build by you. Frames can be built with concrete blocks, timber or bricks and then filled with many organic materials mixed with soil. You will find kits ready for assembling as well as prefabricated plastic containers at almost any gardening center. Now anyone and everyone can quickly and successfully grow their vegetables in raised beds.

1. Excellent Aeration

The older, traditional way to create raised beds is simply to dig up the soil, piling it into rows. You can follow this method and then support the two sides by using solid frames. Otherwise, place your frames in place and then fill them up with compost, farmyard manure mixed with quality soil.

We know that the different parts of plants all need to breathe, and so do the roots. For example during photosynthesis, the leaves take in carbon dioxide and expel oxygen. If your plant sits in compact soil, the roots will suffocate and will not succeed in developing fully. This is because they need proper aeration for their roots to be able to absorb the essential nutrients in the soil. To explain further; the soil bacteria convert the nitrogen in the little air pockets into nitrate salts and nitrate, thus providing the macronutrients for the plant. Without sufficient air, there is a lack of nitrogen and therefore fewer nutrients will be available to the plant.

It is clear that the population of microbes in your vegetable soil must be kept healthy and this is made possible with good aerated soil. The balance of anaerobic and aerobic bacteria should be maintained as they all play their different roles to enhance the fertility of the soil.

2. Good Drainage

Even during a downpour of rain, your raised beds will render good drainage. No wonder this method is so prevalent in the tropics with its heavy rainfall. Because the soil has such a loose texture, water will seep slowly into the bed instead of a making a quick runoff with the accompanying washing away of all fertile topsoil. Furthermore, all the excess water can quickly drain away.

Although most plants do not mind moisture at all, they hate to get their feet wet. Firstly, all that water around their roots will make breathing almost impossible. Secondly, too much moisture will promote fungal and bacterial diseases. Lastly, excess water drenching the soil can change its pH level and raise the acidity. Plants which prefer more neutral or slightly alkaline soil will suffer as a result.

Some plants, for example those that live in bogs are adapted to grow in drenched soil but most plants prefer soil with a twenty five percent-moisture level. Raised beds will not allow water stagnation while at the same time keep your soil quite evenly moist because the water is soaked into the lowest levels of your beds quickly.

3. The Spreading of Roots

Although plant roots can be quite persistent in their effort to grow, they will find it challenging to do so in tightly compacted soil.

In loose soil they can grow and spread out to their hearts' contend. Furthermore, a framed bed will retain the moisture after watering a lot longer than the more traditionally raised beds because the frames prevent water loss on the sides of the beds more effectively. Drying out of the beds can therefore be prevented and good root spreading will follow.

Plants growing in non-raised garden beds generally have a very shallow system of roots since they find it impossible to penetrate through the more compact soil deeper down, unless of course you go to the trouble of tilling the soil deeply before you plant your vegetables. This means that the plant roots are unable to get to the moisture kept in the deeper layers, which in turn may lead to dehydration of the plant when the moisture on the surface evaporates. Well-developed root systems anchor your plants. It also enlarges the potential food source area from which the plant can gather its nutrients and water. Vegetable plants in particular, need enough of both to encourage vigorous growth and maximum yield during their relatively short growing season.

4. Minimum Risk of Compact Soil

A raised bed will not completely deter your smaller pets like dogs and cats from digging and rolling around in your gardening soil, but it definitely will keep humans and larger pets or animals at bay. This will prevent the tamping down of the soil. The ideal width for your raised beds is three to four feet, making it easy for you to do your gardening chores such as weeding, harvesting and fertilizing without having to step onto the beds.

The floods which sometimes occur after a torrential downpour can also compact the soil of cultivated fields. Wet soil is heavy and will sink down and fill all the little air pockets. Once the water has evaporated, you will be left with a dense, hard layer that is not very accommodating for the plants. Raised beds allow the water to drain away much quicker, preventing floods to cause soil compaction.

5. Improved Weed Control

Sick and tired of weeding? A raised bed garden is the answer. In a standard vegetable plot, you will find it hard to get rid of all the frustrating weeds no matter how dedicated you are. They just seem to take over all the time.

When you cultivate the soil for standard vegetable beds, you expose lot of the weed seeds that have been lying dormant underground shielded from the sun. The exposure to sunlight and extra moisture they receive during irrigation will provide them with the opportunity to start sprouting, just what they have been waiting for. Very quickly, they will feed on the nutrient-rich soil prepared for your vegetable plants and begin to flourish.

You can make use of the option to fill your raised beds with relatively weed-free soil and compost. If a few stray weeds appear, your raised beds with its loose soil will make weeding a breeze. A good tip is to fill up your raised beds with as many plants as will grow in it so that they will suffocate and outgrow any stubborn weeds that may try their luck.

6. Easier than Amending Existing Soil

Garden soil greatly varies from area to area; sometimes it is more alkaline and chalky, often it is too acidic and plants will not thrive without your intervention. Vegetables in general like slightly acidic to neutral soil, anything with a pH level of between 5.5 and 7.5. Having said that, there are exceptions. Blueberries and tomatoes, for instance, like more acidic soil while asparagus and broccoli prefer to have their roots in sweeter soil.

The remedy for alkaline soil is to add Sulphur, for acidic soil lime can be added. Sometimes applications have to be repeated a number of times to get the desired effect but a downpour can undo all your hard work in a flash. It is not a simple, straightforward process to change the intrinsic nature of any type of soil.

If you plan to cultivate different kinds of vegetables, raised beds will give you the option of which soil you choose. On top of that, you can now fill up different raised beds with the type of soil each variety of vegetable prefers. The addition of lots of compost, something most gardeners usually do, makes it easier to sustain the soil's neutrality.

7. Garden on Top of Existing Turf

The task of having to dig up and clean the existing turf presently growing on the area you have targeted is just too daunting. Do not despair; raised vegetable beds can be built straight on top of your grass without having to dig up any sods.

Mark your area, and then place multiple layers of cardboard and newspaper on the area. Erect your frames and then simply continue to fill them with grass clippings, soil, sand, decomposed farmyard manure and compost. Plant your seeds or seedlings in this rich mixture and you have started your garden without too much backbreaking labor.

Chapter 1
Planning your Thriving Garden

Remember that for all brand-new Raised Bed gardeners, it might be a case of trial and error to the initial calendar year. It may take the time to find just what fits your requirements. There might be failures along the way, yet we invite you to persevere. It'll be worth all of the efforts as your crops will be bountiful as soon as you succeed.

CONSIDERING PERSONAL CIRCUMSTANCES

We've arrived at the stage of decision making. Here I would like you to look closer in your situation and the way you're able to determine which Raised Bed system will best fit your lifestyle.

1) Space

2) Budget

3) Expertise

4) Timing

SPACE

At the start of the novel, I wrote regarding indoor or outside gardening.

In the event you decide to install outdoors, with no encompassing security, your plants are susceptible to pest infestation.

It may be reduced somewhat in case you've got a greenhouse to cultivate your crops. A conventional glass home or a plastic jar tunnel works well. Should you expand your plants inside, then your plants will not be as prone to fleas. Nonetheless, your space might be more limited inside.

If you're considering growing plants that aren't the standard for the climate, you then may either require a greenhouse or grow inside.

In the event you would like to grow from year crops, then they're going to need particular attention to their surroundings.

In the circumstance, you'll have to consider supplying artificial light, heating system and control the humidity. These cannot be installed at the open and has to be under a protective covering, including a greenhouse, or rather, inside.

BUDGET

The intricacy of the system you've got is also determined by your available budget. You're able to start and ought to start using a tiny, simple method, like Water Staff. As you progress, that is if you will begin to pay more.

You can put all of your gear together by buying each part individually. The only problem you could notice is that you may purchase the incorrect bits and wind up spending more than you initially planned.

You will find readymade kits available with every system. They'll include the specific materials you'll need for this distinct Raised Bed system. At least this way, you may only be purchasing the essential equipment for the job. Although kits tend to be costlier than the DIY option, in the very long term, this may help you save money.

If you're capable of DIY, then you could have the ability to improvise piping and containers. Or perhaps purchase secondhand pieces and pieces, including a pond pump. You have to wash and disinfect everything entirely before use.

EXPERIENCE

Whether you would like to develop specialty crops, or even the simpler ones, like lettuces and herbs, then the Secret to development would be to

1) Humidity

2) Water

3) Heater

4) pH degrees

5) Nutritional advantages

Get these appropriate, and you ought to have a bountiful harvest.

In the first seeding to caring to your origins, from light and all of the various methods of measuring amounts, it comes down to the practice. If you're already a keen gardener, then you'll already have a lot of knowledge required in caring for crops. The expertise of Raised Bed gardening will probably come after, with practice and time. You have to consider these factors, however, before determining which system is most appropriate for you.

TIME

How long spent on your self-indulgent garden is left up to you.

Decide on a method you know will work on your current timetable and way of life. The busier you're, then the more significant your system. It stands to reason that the plants which you have, the time required. Much like any garden, you'll have to watch over plants. Measuring of varying amounts needs to get carried out. Flushing of systems ought to be carried out regularly.

To assist you in picking, I've gone through every Raised Bed procedure to provide a notion of all of these variables: Space, Budget, Expertise, and Time. I hope that this can allow you to select which Raised Bed system in the event the perfect one for you.

WHICH SYSTEM WORKS BEST FOR YOU?

DRIP SYSTEM

Space

A fundamental drip process is attainable for any novice. It will occupy a bit more space since there are two big containers. The machine may sit on a desk.

Budget

There's much more equipment to purchase utilizing this technique. You'll have to have at least a circulating pump, a timer, and a tube. You'll also need a trickle manifold. In case the budget is tight, then you can make tiny holes in the machine instead. This system demands a growing medium. It may be expensive to operate than the Water Staff, or even Ebb and Flow, programs. It is because it creates a more efficient utilization of these nutrients, hence using less. This might not make much difference to a bigger garden. To gain from that, you'd require at least 10+ crops from the computer system.

Expertise

It's a bit complex to establish. This procedure is much more complicated than Water Staff, which may be carried out in one bucket. It's also more

Complex compared to Ebb and Flow to establish. If you're just beginning, it may be better to purchase a ready-made kit with all of the ideal elements in 1 area. Be conscious that tubing may get blocked with all the surplus minerals in your nutrient liquid. Be cautious of the since your harvest will dry up and perish from not getting any water. A higher skill level is required for this program. You will need a simple comprehension of balancing the attention of nutrition. Besides, you require a fantastic understanding of how frequently the pump needs to be off and on. Get these incorrect, and your crops will suffer. When it isn't sufficient, then the origins might be stunted, or perhaps worse, then dry outside. When it's a lot, the roots can clot or develop a parasite. This system is dependent upon electric power. Ensure that you check it occasionally and understand what to do when it goes away.

Time

There are a couple of maintenance jobs that will require focus. The stream of nourishment should be nicely balanced. Verify the pipes frequently so that they do not get blocked. If the electricity cut off, then the entire machine will probably come to a halt. You must check it regularly because it's possible to lose your whole harvest.

Every one of these issues is extremely valuable to the achievement of your backyard. Failure on any of these points, along with your harvest, will perish.

EBB AND FLOW

Space

Much the same in distance requirements into the Drip System. The expanding tray ought to be sitting on a desk using the entire reservoir container beneath so it could make full use of gravity. This program works well inside.

Budget

To put up this system, you'll have to purchase some simple equipment, like a pump, tube, timer, and moderate.

Experience

It's not difficult to keep as soon as you get the hang of this. But, it may be a bit complex to establish. If DIY isn't something, then you will find readymade kits to purchase containing whatever you want.

Assessing temperature and pH levels isn't so crucial for this technique. You still ought to measure these amounts, nevertheless not as frequently.

Time

Nutrient water at the reservoir may require changing every 7-10 days. Additionally, the system will require a thorough wash, with hydrogen peroxide, even following a crop. It's ideal for testing pH levels every day, so it's possible to fix them if desired. You have to inspect regularly the pump is functioning, and the tube doesn't become obstructed.

NUTRIENT FILM TECHNIQUE

Space

The increase tray is generally a gulley or station; therefore, it could be lengthy. Besides, you need room to get a tank that retains the nutrient-enriched H20. Again, it's wise if the increased tray is located on top along with the reservoir beneath. Like most Raised Bed methods, if it's maintained small, it could be installed indoors.

Budget

As it's a constant flow method, you'll require a pump; however, a timer isn't vital. It's an affordable way to begin your Raised Bed growing, yet it's also somewhat complicated, so take note. No medium is demanded. The crops are stored in baskets, at a lid with pockets, so the origins hang out and get to the station of water. To guarantee the reservoir water is ventilated, an air rock fed through an air purification pump is a great option.

Experience

Setting up could be tricky. The increase channels will need to be in an angle so that the water runs from 1 end to another. In case the corner isn't right, then the crops can flood or shut out. You'll have to understand how to measure pH and temperature degrees since these require checking daily.

Time

NFT isn't hard to keep with very little work necessary to keep it functioning well. The tremendous job is substituting the nutrient-enriched H20. It has to be performed every two weeks to make sure the crops are adequately fed. Once harvesting, your own body will require a thorough clean outside. The developing station and reservoir may develop with dangerous germs. Suspended roots may grow a long time and limit the circulation of water. If that is the situation, then you can cut them without damaging the crops. It's crucial to maintain the water temperature cool at approximately 68F/20C.

WATER CULTURE

Space

You can begin with as small as the distance necessary to get a 5-gallon bucket. Everything which you require can be confined to a single container. It can be complicated if you want to expand the machine after. One bucket, nutrient safety, and a lid with pockets inside are all you want to begin on this Raised Bed system. If you don't develop individual crops in containers, together with all the roots suspended from the water, you then do not even require a developing medium.

Budget

It may be the least costly system to establish.

It may run with no moderate by hanging out your crops via a hole cut at a lid. It may be better to utilize little baskets to your roots so that the plants possess some way of support. You'll have to purchase moderate if you decide to utilize plant pots for every plant. Unless you're operating a bigger machine, you don't require a water heater.

Should you start small with the entire one container, then you can develop 1-4 plants at precisely the same system. It is precisely what I recommend to the beginner. Start small, and then as you get expertise, expand your own body.

Chapter 2
Building the Raised Bed Garden

Now that you have chosen your location to build your permanent raised bed, you need to gather all your supplies together, and this can be done in an afternoon quickly depending on what you have decided to construct it out of.

What You Will Need:

•Hammer (with suitable weight)

•Tape measure

•Pencil

•Saw (circular or miter)

•Drill or impact drill

•Galvanized screws 3" long

•Wood

Considerations When Choosing Materials

•Durability

•Cost-effectiveness

•Toxicity

•Aesthetics

•Environmental impact

•Portability

•Maintenance

•Duration of construction

Choosing what you will construct your raised bed has a number of factors and considerations, but ultimately it's your choice to suit your budget and the size of the bed. Reclaimed or recycled materials are popular as they are usually the most affordable; they have a low environmental impact, as they don't require any forestry, manufacture, or any long-distance transport. If you check locally on free sites, salvage yards, or even the local refuse center regularly, you will undoubtedly find reusable materials to use; you just may need to be patient!

I will elaborate below on the different qualities of wood you can use and how this could affect your plants, but I would urge you to do your own research on the different materials to use and find what works best for you and your plot. When I started making my first raised bed garden, I went to my local hardware store and bought some timber and was overwhelmed with the choice! Using untreated or organically treated wood is what I now would recommend to build your raised garden. If the budget stretches to it, using a naturally rot-resistant wood such as redwood or cedar is a great option and gives a great aesthetic too. They are extremely durable materials to use, will last 15 years, at least depending on your weather conditions.

Different Materials to Build Your Raised Bed

Wood or Scaffolding Boards

Some pressure-treated wood is toxic, so it's worth researching and using wood that is not. Use wooden planks that have been pressure treated with Tanalith E, which is an organic preservative, perfectly safe to use around your crops.

For reference, the most toxic pressure treated wooden planks CCA (Chromated Copper Arsenate) can be determined by its greenish hue around staple-like depressions. But to make it more confusing for the consumer, not all types of CCA treated wood have these indicators! This can be mixed up with pressure-treated wood which has been treated with ACQ (Alkaline Copper Quaternary) as they BOTH have the distinctive green hue. The ACQ treated wood is, however, considered safe to use. The only accurate method to determine if it is CCA treated and so toxic, or ACQ treated and considered to be non-toxic is to buy an arsenic testing kit and test it yourself for peace of mind.

The lumber we can purchase now will generally be treated with ACQ and another compound CA-B (Copper Azole) they both have a fungicide and copper but not any arsenic. The purpose of the copper compound is to deter pests and insects, and the fungicide in the compound is there to restrict the soil fungi migrating into the wood. The fungicide in AQC is quat, which is used in swimming pool chemicals and disinfectants. CA-B is a fungicide, which is used on food crops and is made up of copper and tebuconazole. In short, copper-infused lumber to use as a project such as a raised garden bed is considered safe to grow food crops.

If you have existing wood in your garden that you are thinking of using for your raised bed, it's worth considering testing the wood to see if it has been treated with CCA. The continued migration of the arsenic into your plot, even if you are not using the wood in your raised bed, will affect the whole area eventually, migrating into your fertile soil for your crops.

Pinewood is another alternative, and the attraction is the cost, which is much lower than say redwood or cedar; however, it will not last as long as such hardy woods. But it's easy to source and easy to manage too. The wood you select will, of course, differ significantly from region to region, but the best choice and quite often the most cost-efficient, is locally sourced, with an FSC (Forest Stewardship Council) certification. It doesn't have the great aesthetic that hardwoods give, and you will have to pay more for organically treated pine. Personally, I wouldn't use treated pine unless it was safe to grow my crops and my thoughts are if you do, it will be at the back of your mind that your product may be contaminated due to high percentage of chemicals used, I believe it's better to start as you mean to carry on.

Cedar, redwood, Juniper, and Yew are all naturally rot-resistant and extremely durable and long-lasting and do give a great look and finish to your garden if your budget allows. There is a reason many choose these types of wood and find them superior, their durability and versatility, as well as their aesthetic and the fact they are easy to work with. The downside is the cost is usually twice the price of say pine; also, they are not very sustainable as hardwoods are slower growers.

When visiting your lumber yard, it's a great practice to note what sizes the lumber comes in; that way you can tailor your raised bed to this exact size minimizing any waste cuts. 8-foot lengths by 4-foot widths are a perfect size for me, but this may not work for you.

Wooden Frame Kits

Some will be reading this thinking how lazy can you be, but some people just don't have the time and ability to source materials to self-build; you can find these at a lot of hardware or garden stores and, of course, Amazon. They are pre-made garden bed kits that come in a variety of sizes, are well priced, and easy to construct. The downsides are some of the quality, certainly of the wood isn't always the greatest (you don't always know the country of origin either), so it may not be durable and long-lasting. Also, once constructed and filled, you may find because of poor durability and strength, you may see some bowing under the strain of the moist earth. Indeed, if it's starting to bow at that point, rest assured on the first torrential downpour, it will worsen. Not all are built this way, though, so if this is the option you want, have a good hunt around and look at reviews, etc. to make sure it is right for your project.

Brick Built Raised Beds

These can be time-consuming and require some skill to build; however, they are built to last and will serve you well for years to come, plus if built well, they look stunning in your garden.

You will need a string, a spirit level (use it at every given opportunity to get perfectly level walls!) bricks, and a hard-core base of rubble. Don't forget to leave regular gaps between brick joints to allow room for drainage; you can go ahead at the end to cover these holes with mesh to stop any clogging.

Another alternative to brick is to use blocks or concrete panels, which will require rendering to give a polished finish; these methods do offer good insulation for your plants at a reasonably low cost too.

The downside, though, is if you needed to move your bed, it would be troublesome to relocate. Also, you may find over time; it could crack or sink.

Railway Sleeper Raised Beds

A very popular choice is to use old rustic looking railway sleepers which give a great aesthetic to any garden, however most authentic or vintage ones will have been treated with tar and creosote, which will inevitably be transferred into your nutrient-rich soil and affect the quality of your crops.

They can be pricey to purchase, although if you hunt around, you can find a good deal at salvage yards, also not all are the same size, so some adaptation will be required to get the sizing right for your raised bed.

If this is the look you want for your raised bed, I would seriously consider softwood sleepers that have been treated with eco-friendly preservatives. The bonus is no nasty chemicals to tarnish your crops and also lighter material to handle while constructing, a bit more pricey but overall the better option of the two.

Now you have decided on what you are building with and sourced the materials you now need to prepare the area before you actually build the bed.

When preparing the land you need to ensure that the area is reasonably level, don't worry too much if you are thinking of shallow root system crops but for deeper root system crops (carrots, parsnips, etc.) it would be worth breaking the soil surface on the area and digging to appropriately 30cm depth, removing any rocks and debris that would hinder healthy root growth. But if you are building your bed no deeper than 14-16 inches high, then I recommend lifting the grass and sod from the surface and inverting it before construction.

Building Your Raised Bed

After measuring your site, and inverting the turf. You can apply a landscape fabric this, however, has proven only to offer modest weed prevention. It has also managed to prevent earthworms from being able to get to the nutrient-rich soil to help aerate said soil. Also, the fact using landscape fabric may be detrimental to the overall drainage of the raised bed. In its place, I recommend using newspaper or cardboard, which will break down.

Using string and stakes mark out the dimensions of your raised bed. Using a spirit level at all times will ensure you get a straight, even raised bed. If you have ordered the exact size for your raised bed from the hardware store, go ahead and begin to use the screws to attach the timber lengths together. If not, cut to size and attach. Don't forget to measure twice and cut once!

Screws will last longer and are easier if you want to move the raised bed at any time; however, nails are easier to work with and quicker.

If you find you have difficulty getting the screws in, you can pre-drill the holes. Always use galvanized fixtures to protect from corrosion if your budget allows.

If you are concerned with small rodents being able to get into your construction, you can opt to line the bed with a metal hardware cloth or mesh (1/4 or 1/2“) to the bottom of the bed. Using staples to attach is the easiest method.

Avoiding the use of plastic, if possible, as the toxins can leach into the soil and contaminate your plants; it will also contribute to discouraging the much-needed earthworms and insects and have a detrimental effect on your drainage.

Here is an excellent example of how to build a great raised garden bed from Off Grid With Doug and Stacy on YouTube http://b

Chapter 3
Which Vegetables Grow in Raised Beds

If you plant your raised bed garden correctly, you can get amazing crops of vegetables, flowers, and herbs with very little effort compared to what you must do in traditional gardening.

These types of gardens have an important role in the landscape of the home. They feature framed areas above the ground, and often have wooden frames around the area. They have an increased ability to drain away excess water, and eliminate compacted soil. In addition, you can add soil nutrients as necessary to help your plants be the best they can be. This allows gardeners to plant a variety of plants in their garden.

Most plants will work well in raised bed gardens. The exception is those plants that are large or have very deep roots or sprawling top growth. Other plants that don't work in raised beds are those that are top-heavy and tall and therefore need to be firmly anchored.

Since the plants in your raised beds will be sharing soil, light, fertilizer, and water, you should make sure to choose plants with similar or the same requirements for growth and development.

As far as size, moderately tall plants work well. Also, trailing plants or smaller plants work quite well in raised bed gardens, and can be planted together. Planting in raised beds is just another type of container gardening, and therefore basically requires you to follow the same rules. Plant your tallest plants in the center of your bed, and go down to the smaller plants near the edge. Plant the trailing plants along the edges, so they spill over.

Vegetables are pretty easy to grow in raised beds. You can maximize the amount of yield you get from your crops by planting the summer plants as soon as the spring ones have been harvested and fall ones as soon as the summer ones have been harvested. Since the fertilizer and soil are easier to control, you can plant vegetables and plants closer together than in a traditional garden.

In addition, raised bed gardens are being used to raise tropical houseplants as annuals. The raised garden beds can be a spectacular addition to your backyard décor.

As far as flowering plants go, you can raise both annuals and perennials in your raised garden. You should choose annuals that match the availability of sunlight in your area. The growing conditions offered in the raised bed garden seriously increase the growth of the annuals, so make sure that you allow enough room for them to grow. Annuals will flourish in the rich soil offered in the raised bed garden.

Perennials will give your garden a more permanent addition. They will flower year after year and can form the basis for your raised bed garden. You can add perennials to create a low maintenance garden that requires very little work through the seasons. To achieve constant color and flowering, you should choose plants that bloom at various times of the year.

Raised bed gardens are great for vegetable gardening because they offer a neat area for planting. The rich soil will ensure that you have a prosperous harvest, providing that you have placed them in such a way that there is room for growth. Make sure that you read all your labels so that you can decide on the best placement for the plants. An added benefit of the raised bed garden is that it keeps pests out- the frame provides a base to which you can place poles to attach fencing.

Peas

Peas work well in raised garden beds, according to the National Gardening Association. The raised design helps drain the excess water away and allows gardeners to plant earlier. You should plant peas after the last frost of the winter.

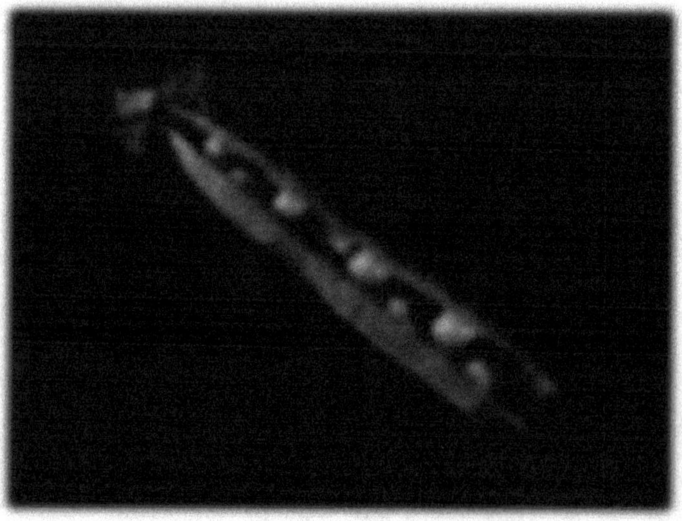

Peppers

According to the National Gardening Association, peppers grow quite well in raised bed gardens, especially if they're really wet. This is because of the drainage and the warmer temperatures offered by raised bed gardens. It's best to plant them after the last spring frost, but they can be started inside earlier and then moved outside in order to create an earlier harvest.

Eggplant

Like peppers, raised beds are great for growing eggplants. They like lots of sun as they grow and will do exceptionally well with a layer of mulch around the base of the plants in order to prevent the growth of weeds. Eggplants have beautiful purple flowers that make your vegetable garden especially attractive.

Okra

Okra grows quite well in raised beds and does really well next to peppers and eggplants. According to the National Gardening Association, you should plant okra from a seed. It doesn't do well with frost and doesn't do well in a really hot climate either.

Another great addition to raised bed gardens are herbs. They grow just as well as the vegetables and annuals will. The extra organic material and the soil looseness allow the roots to spread quite nicely. When the roots spread, the plant can better absorb nutrients and moisture from the soil. Herbs can be paired with vegetables or annuals, or can be planted all on their own. You should disperse those strong-smelling herbs throughout the garden to repel insets. In addition, you will attract bees and butterflies, which will keep the pests to a minimal level.

Tomatoes

Tomatoes are one of the easier vegetables to grow, but there are still environmental factors you will need to plan for and take into consideration during the spring and summer growing season. Growing a full and healthy set of tomatoes is accomplished by considering issues of sun exposure, watering, and soil health. Location and Soil

Tomato plants like full sun and they always should get several hours of sun a day. Little sun means little tomatoes or even non-producing plants.

If you are growing from seed start them indoors or in a greenhouse about 6 weeks before the last frost. Plant out into garden beds when frosts are over.

Tomatoes enjoy very fertile soil and will respond well to organic matter mixed into the beds. One of the mistakes that new tomato growers often make is watering the plants too much and not giving the soil enough attention. Till about 5 or 6 inches of soil, and to mix compost into the area.

Types of Tomatoes

Tomatoes are usually referred to as "hybrids" or "heirlooms," different types of tomatoes offer different benefits. While an heirloom tomato has a long history of tasty tomato production, hybrid tomato plants will usually offer more fruit each season.

Hybrid plants are also usually much more resistant to disease. Certain types of hybrids have even been grown to be resistant to a specific type of disease, which may be helpful for a person with a garden in a disease-prone area.

Watering

A tomato plant should be watered at its base and its best not to get the leaves wet. Unless temperatures reach near 100 degrees during the day, the plants may be watered every 2 or 3 days.

These plants won't tolerate soggy conditions which are another plus for using a raised bed to plant them in. If you set it up properly with the optimum soil profile, then drainage won't be an issue.

Cucumbers

Because they are so easy to grow, include cucumbers when you are starting with your raised bed vegetable garden. Most cucumbers are of the vine type and send out runners, but there are also some varieties of bush cucumbers and they generally fall into 2 category types...pickling and slicing cucumbers.

Cucumbers also like soil that is rich in organic matter and is well drained but since them like the sun which tends to dry out the soil, you'll need to use mulch to preserve the soil's moisture. It is better to use black or brown mulch as this will help to retain moisture best as well as keeping the soil warm.

Cucumbers grow as bushes or vines and can be planted in containers, in rows, raised beds, or even vertically. Bush varieties grow well in containers while the vines will need a trellis which is easier to use in the garden.

Like the other vegetables in the cucumber family (the cucurbits), for example zucchini, pumpkins, and melons, they are heavy feeders and need to be supplemented well with nutrients. Work organic matter (compost, well-rotted manure) into the soil before to planting, and fertilizers will not be needed early on. But when they begin to blossom and fruit appears; add a balanced soluble fertilizer to help them produce their potential of thriving cucumbers in large number.

Cucumbers are ready for harvest in about 60 to 70 days after planting. Cucumbers need to be harvested when they are young and tender as they get bitter as they grow bigger. The slicing type cucumbers can be harvested when they are 6 to 8 inches long while pickling types are gathered at around 5 inches.

Carrots

Carrots are usually grown from seed though you can buy punnets (small light basket) of seedlings. It is much more cost effective to sow seeds. Spread the seeds thinly so the carrots will not be crowded, and as seedlings emerge, remove any weak and spindly plants.

Carrots require a lot of sun so choose a place that gets ample sunlight. Work in your soil amendment until it is mixed evenly but at the same time not overworked into a fine powder which can form a crust. Learn more about these popular root veggies.

How to Grow Pumpkins

Growing pumpkins is a lot like growing Zucchini's in that they are both low-to-the-ground growers with vines that can spread 4-6 inches a day. The yellow flowers that sprout out on these vines in about 40 days or so, develop into the gourd-like vegetable.

The art of pumpkin growing can sometimes seem like a dark art to the uninitiated, but the fact is that it can be a lot of fun to learn how to grow them in a way that both maximizes their size and flavor.

The first decision that you need to make is whether you are growing the pumpkin to be used as a lantern at Halloween, or for eating in pumpkin pie. The reason is that different types of pumpkin are better for each use.

If you want a real monster pumpkin that you can carve out a face on and discard the innards, then you will generally be better off buying a Variety like a Howden.

Chapter 4
Planting and Maintaining Your Raised Bed Garden

Once you have seeded your raised bed garden and have raised the seedlings into young plants, you are still going to need to pay careful attention to your plants and their needs. As the gardener looking after these beds it is up to you to properly water and fertilize your plants. It is up to you to repair the frame and amend the soil. And it is up to you to watch out for pests and to prevent disease from entering into your garden. While you could skip these steps, your garden won't stay healthy unless you follow through with them all.

But while all of these are necessary, they aren't difficult. In fact, raised bed gardens are easier to maintain than traditional gardens are and depending on the size of your beds you may not even have to bend down to work on them anymore. The height of a raised bed makes it easier to maintain and the contained environment means there is less that needs to be checked. We'll figure out how to maintain ours starting with the soil before moving on to fertilizing, watering, and pest protection.

Amending the Soil

As gardeners, our goal should be to keep our garden as healthy as can be so that it continues to produce fantastic results year after year. But doing this shouldn't mean spending a lot of money. A little bit of attention from time to time will allow you to keep the same soil in your raised garden bed for years without a problem? To look after our soil, we're going to amend it occasionally and make sure it is protected throughout the winter. By taking care of it before the start of winter and just after the end, you'll be able to keep your soil healthy for many seasons to come. You should still check on the quality of the soil when you can but this won't be necessary when the following steps are heeded.

When we mixed up our soil for our raised beds, we start from a base of 33% compost. This means that there are lots of nutrients in our garden soil to begin with. But as each harvest passes, there are going to be fewer and fewer nutrients in the soil. You should add compost either after you finish harvesting or in early spring when you start to prepare the beds. While this is one way to get lots of nutrients into the soil, we'll also be using a liquid fertilizer in a few moments and this will ensure that there are tons of nutrients available to the plants.

When you or I eat, we stop after we get full. Plants can't do this. If there are too many nutrients in the soil then they may suffer nutrient burn. The edges of leaves will gradually curl up like the legs of a dead spider and it'll start to change colors. It's an ugly sight. You may need to check the pH level of the garden bed to make sure it is still within the proper levels that it was supposed to be. If there are too many nutrients then you will want to water as normal but skip a fertilizer application or two so that the soil is flushed out a bit first.

The organic elements in the soil will break down over time. When this happens, they start to stick together much tighter and the pathways through the soil start to get blocked up. This makes the soil tougher for roots to push through while also blocking access to oxygen and slowing down the drainage speed. As you water your garden throughout the first year, be mindful of how long it takes to dry out and the way the water soaks into it. When you first start, it will seem a little odd to be watching the water this closely but over time it will tell you about the quality of the soil. When it starts to slow down and really change, typically after two years or more, then you will know what is happening. At the beginning of the new growing season, you can either amend the soil by adding more sandy minerals to it or you can replace the soil with a fresh batch. It can be expensive to replace the soil every few years constantly. Amending is the much cheaper way to go but you need to be careful and take it slow. You could completely wreck the soil if you added too much of one thing in without mixing it around and getting a feeling for the texture.

Winter is a big change in the weather and you need to prepare your raised garden beds to weather the storms. First off, most gardeners yank their plants out at the end of the season so that they can replant in the following spring. This is a good idea but you should only cut away the above-soil part of the plant. Remove any root vegetables as well but you want to leave the roots. Over the course of the winter they will turn into nutritious compost for your next crop. Speaking of compost, if you decide to add compost to the bed at the end of the growing season then you should make a layer of it on top, then cover this with a layer of mulch. This will make it so weeds can't get in, plus it will allow the compost to amend the soil and replenish many of the nutrients that were spent that summer.

If you aren't going to be mulching your raised garden beds then you should consider covering them using a strong plastic tarp. This will protect the soil and act in the place of mulch. It won't look quite as nice but if you are in an area where it snows a lot then you know that everything looks the same when it's buried in white fluff. It will be cheaper and far faster to put a tarp over your raised garden bed but mulching is the way to go if you are going to add compost before the winter. If you mulch, you can still use the tarp but it is rather redundant to use both methods.

By following these simple steps you can keep your soil lasting years. Checking on it throughout the season is important but making sure you prepare it for the winter and then "wake it up" again in the spring, it'll last you quite a while. The health of your soil is an investment well worth making. If you ignore it, you will find that it gets harder and harder to grow anything in your raised beds. You might think there is a problem with the bed while it is the soil at fault.

Fertilizing Your Raised Bed Garden

When you start seedlings indoors, you begin to fertilize them. When seedlings start to sprout outdoors, you fertilize them. As your plants grow and mature, you fertilize them. It is only just before you harvest any edible vegetables that you stop fertilizing them because you don't want to add any more liquid to the soil. Fertilizing your plants is an absolute must if you want beautiful flowers or large yields.

Fertilizer comes in two types. There are fertilizers such as manure which can be added to and then mixed throughout the soil. A fertilizer like this is a good application at the start of spring or end of fall. However, we can also mix in compost as a top layer with a blanket of mulch to protect our beds over the winter and add nutrients back into the soil. So we're not going to worry about fertilizers that mix into the soil. Instead, we're going to stick with liquid fertilizer.

Some gardeners brew what is called manure tea, which sounds as tasty as it smells. Another form of fertilizer is created by crushing comfrey until it oozes a sap which you distill in water and then feed your plants. For our purposes we will be sticking to the store bought liquid fertilizers but even here we have two options. The first option is to buy a premixed fertilizer. These are ones with the NPK ratio listed on them in numeric form like 30-30-30. If you get confused by the numbers on fertilizer bottles then don't worry, we'll cover that in a moment. But if you do get confused by them then we're better off buying a premixed fertilizer rather than purchasing the raw materials to make our own. Whatever we purchase will still be diluted in water but the package can be read and it will have instructions for you to follow.

We've already referred to these numbers as the NPK ratio, so let's dig into what that means. Plants need a bunch of nutrients and micronutrients. The macronutrients they need are nitrogen, phosphorus, potassium, calcium, magnesium, and sulfur. Also included in these are hydrogen, oxygen, and carbon. Micronutrients for them include iron, manganese, copper, zinc, boron, and molybdenum. If you are adding compost to your soil and keeping it healthy then you are going to have most of these nutrients in place in the soil. This is refreshing since trying to balance all of these would be a lot of effort. We have to worry about six primarily. Hydrogen is found in water and we provide plenty of water to our plants throughout the growing season. We make sure that the soil drains quickly and this also lets both oxygen and carbon get to the roots and so half of the necessary nutrients are provided simply by paying attention to the soil and watering your plants.

The other three important nutrients for us to worry about are nitrogen (N), phosphorus (P), and potassium (K). Together, these three nutrients play the biggest role in the development of your plant. Nitrogen is used to make the leaves of the plant grow faster and come in more fully. Phosphorus is used by the plants to strengthen the roots and make them grow big and strong. Potassium is a general nutrient which is used in multiple functions of the plant that are required for it to properly use and distribute energy from the sun and the soil. The three numbers on the soil refer to these three elements. This is the NPK ratio or the NPK balance and it tells you the percentage of nitrogen, phosphorus, and potassium in the fertilizer. It will always be in that order, NPK; so many labels don't bother labeling the numbers on the front.

Chapter 5
Crop Rotation and Seeding Techniques Succession

It is extremely important that you practice crop rotation in your raised beds to prevent the build-up of pests and diseases in the soil. As you are using raised beds these are going to be low initially, but if you grow the same crop year after year in the same bed then you will encounter problems as the pests or diseases targeting that particular crop build up.

Crop rotation is key to successfully growing vegetables because not only does it reduce pests and diseases, but it helps to ensure that the soil retains vital nutrients and micro-organisms which are beneficial to your plants. Add in succession planting and you further help the soil whilst getting even more out of your vegetable plot!

Crop rotation is perfectly natural, having been practiced by farmers for thousands of years as it is vital to maintain soil quality and interrupt the lifecycle of pests. However, remember that this only applies to annual plants and not your perennial plants such as asparagus, fruit bushes and so on. These stay in the same place year after year, but you will have to work the soil and many people move them when they have outlived their usefulness or reached the end of their life. Applying manure or fertilizer once or twice during a growing season is often enough to keep these permanent plants happy.

Crop rotation helps to reduce the severity and incidences of diseases such as tomato or potato blight, onion/leek rust, and many others, as well as crop specific pests. As you do not grow the same crop in the same soil season after season, the diseases do not have the opportunity to build up. Some pests or diseases will live in the soil for a few years and by rotating your crop you ensure these pests die out before they have a chance to establish themselves.

Like many things in existence, should you like to succeed, you need to begin putting the foundation for achievement in an early phase growing crops is comparable? You need to begin with the safest, most vigorous seedlings to acquire healthy, effective crops since they older there's certainly a term in agriculture which Says: "Start. Having a great seedling to reach a more healthy plant; begin using a bad, Feeble seedling to Finish at a less Effective plant" Optimum Ecological conditions may considerably affect the wellbeing and productivity of this harvest significant factors which affect seed germination comprise fever, water, and oxygen, and all of that can be significant to commence rapid development and growth of the embryo at the seed to start a wholesome lifetime of their plant.

Many seed catalogs provide Info on the best temperature ranges, such as seed germination. They frequently provide tastes of their dirt conditions and also mild for optimal plant expansion follow these hints carefully. Soil conditions normally refer to drainage, and which directly affects oxygen amounts to seed germination and subsequent Expansion. The Kind of substrate plays a significant function for Its greatest germination of seeds since it has to consume sufficient hydration, However in the same time provide good aeration as oxygen is still necessary from the germination procedure with Raised Bed substrates, Such oxygen amounts will probably be supplied with Most of the substrates, but for greater moisture retention you may utilize a perlite or coco coir Moderate, whereas Greater "well-drained" substrates refer to vermiculite, Rough sand, and perlite.

Consistently watch the percent germination provided on seed bundles to ascertain the number of new seeds to sow for the proper last variety of crops. For example, if the germination test suggests 85 Percent, multiply the Reverse of the Amount times. That the Closing number of Crops (Emails Gram, 30 Crops) necessary (100/85 × 30 plants = 35 plants). It's also an excellent practice to sow at least 10 Percent more seeds than you desire for transplanting because lets you choose the very top buds for transplanting and Climbing on. Applying this case Afterward, (35 + 10 Percent × 35 = 39) sow 39 seeds. The Exact Amount of seeds to sow per growth block or tray mobile varies for different Plants, particularly herbs, which are sown in clusters or bunches. Many seeds, including lettuce, Can Be Found in raw type and pelleted type in certain Instances, seeds Might be Bought as clusters or even as noodle seed to Alleviate sowing and enhance germination. From the demonstration on respective plants which follows, a manual is provided for the Number of seeds to Float per Block

ARUGULA

Arugula seed is rather small, using a seed diameter of about 1 mm (roughly 1 32). This little seed is tough to sow a certain amount of seeds correctly. Many seed businesses make seed clusters of approximately 12 seeds trapped with water-soluble glue. Normally approximately 10--12 seeds each block are the right density. Or, the seedlings could be emptied upon germination by cutting on down the excess ones away close to their foundation using a spoonful. Be cautious not to harm those to be stored if thinning. Sow the seeds at Oasis or stone wool cubes or a petite combination in 72-celled compact trays. In baskets or beds of perlite, substrate sows the seeds into the container Should you would like to transplant out of cubes to nutrient film technique (NFT) or even raft civilization do this 14--18 day after sowing the seeds. Optimum temperature range for germination of arugula is 65--75°F (18--24°C) along with pH between

6.0 and 6.8. Most vegetable plants such as a pH in 6.2 to 6.5. Germination requires from 5 to seven times. Utilize raw water to your initial seven times till they achieve about an inch, and then utilize a half-strength nutrient alternative before they enjoy complete mild to partial shade. It requires approximately 3--4 months to harvest and maybe chosen just two times afterward at three weeks --4-week periods. Since the plants grow, they get bitterer, so it's better to substitute them following three cuttings.

BOK CHOY

Sow bok choy from rock wool or even Oasis cubes and then transplant them into NFT, raft civilization, or plant creatures in 21--25 days. Sow one seed each block or even longer, narrow them into a plant in 12 days old with scissors whenever they're about 3/4. Top Geminate the seed using uncooked water to your very first eight days, after which a half-strength nutrient alternative before transplanting. Optimum germination temperatures are between 75°F and also 83°F (24--28°C). The round, black, and bok choy seed is marginally more than 1 16. in diameter and, consequently, is simpler to manage than this of arugula.

LETTUCE

Lettuce, because I'm certain you're aware, is a cool-season harvest, so reduced temperatures tend to be more beneficial for this, temperatures out of 60--65°F (16--18°C) are greatest for germination and expansion. The carrot seed could eventually become dormant in elevated temperatures, particularly previously 68°F (20°C).

Utilizing pelleted carrot seed extends the temperature range for germination by beating dormancy caused by elevated temperatures. Maintain pelleted and uncooked lettuce seed trendy and dry in a fridge and use it inside a year, particularly pelleted seeds. For both indoor and subtropical growing usage, heat-tolerant types are resistant to bolting (going to seed) and also tip burn (browning of outer borders of leaves). Start lettuce in Oasis or rock wool cubes. I favor rock wool cubes since they don't split apart as readily as Oasis during transplanting, particularly within raft civilization in which it's essential for your seedling block to stay intact since the cubes are thrown somewhat to match to the planting holes of their boards.

We're matching square cubes into round holes of their planks. The principle of square pegs in round holes applies. With a few NFT stations, the holes are both squares, and also, the cubes match little attempt. The seedlings should be transplanted at 18--21 days old to their generation boards or stations. Here is a process to raise the generation efficiency of your developing system from using two transplant phases.

Having a raft culture method utilizes a 2 feet × 4 feet board comprising 72 seedlings (six rows of 12 plants) and transplant that the very first time in 10--12 times as the seedlings achieves their third true-leaf phase. Determined by just how many crops you're growing, you can decrease how big the first-stage transplant to two feet × 2 feet using 36 crops. A rule-of-thumb is that the nursery region ought to be approximately 20 percent of their entire machine. The seedlings are transplanted for their second-stage (closing generation) planks in their fourth true-leaf phase (roughly 18--21 days from sowing) approximately 2 --10 days before transplanting. At this point, you will find 18 plants (three rows of six crops) per two feet × 4 feet final generation plank. The lettuce will probably be prepared to harvest inside a second 24--30 times, creating the complete cycle approximately 45 days from sowing.

Together With NFT, the process resembles Plants have been seeded in Oasis or rock wool cubes (phase 1) and therefore are transplanted for the first time in particular nursery NFT stations that have plant holes in two. Inside the station and stations are split in 4. Center to center. A 12-ft station matches 72 Control Again, ratio the nursery trays in 20 percent of their total generation capability Start the seedlings in 1. Rockwool cubes (200 cubes/pad) or Oasis 1" lean cut" Horticubes (276 cubes/pad).

Grow these seedlings from the trays around the propagation seat for approximately 18 days before attaching into the nursery station (s) (phase 2). Maintain them at the nursery station for approximately 10--12 times (28--30 days from sowing) before alerting them into the completing stations (phase 3). Inside 20--25 days crop the adult lettuce in the developing (completing) channels providing you 14 plants annually.

In consequence, the carrot just occupies the creation region for 20--25 times; that's efficacy in using your growing distance! The closing generation interval depends upon the total amount of lighting and daylight length. This can change somewhat to get a garden greenhouse because of this year. Utilizing supplemental lights to prolong the day to 14 hours ought to assist in attaining shorter generation intervals.

LETTUCE SALAD COMBINES

Germinate the seeds for lettuce between 60°F along with 65°F (15.5--18°C). Harvest over three months is cutting on the very best grips using scissors or electrical knives. Permit three months or not involving harvests to get re-growth of those leaves. This harvesting could be replicated a few times to get a total of 3 harvests involving harvest fluctuations.

BASIL

Basils germinate quickly, generally in 4--5 times at temperatures between 75°F along with 80°F (24--27°C). Utilize any well-drained substrate like a pearlite or even coco coir combination if climbing them in pearlite containers or beds. Additionally, they germinate and grow nicely in rock wool and also Oasis cubes should you want to transplant into an NFT or even raft culture system. When the very first true leaves seem to start with a half-strength nutrient option to nourish them. I've discovered that sowing 3--4 seeds at a plug or block to transplant over three months provides a nice bunch of basil plants.

Space them around 6. × 6. From the creation region, Spacing them as the lettuce will probably allow their growing rapidly to a bushy type of numerous stalks. Don't let them blossom unless you especially need the blossoms as this aging of these crops induces them to become woody eventually. No matter rotates the harvest every three weeks after creating several harvests. Otherwise, to get one crop, as is generally true for NFT or even raft culture creation, eliminate the crops whenever they hit six months --8. in elevation.

Chapter 6
Irrigation

Watering the garden is not as easy as putting on the pants and leaving it to run for some time. Recall the Four Golden Rules of Irrigation as you water or irrigate your garden:

A. Consider where to drink.

B. Know how much water is needed.

C. Know how easily this water can be added.

D. About how many cycles to drink.

Factors influencing these laws include:

A. Climate

B. Soil type

C. Plant type

Note that the primary feeder roots of any seed extend 1 1/2 to 3 times the width of the surface of the plant, where the rest of the water is drained. Watering the whole root is essential to sustain a safe, well-spread root system. The rest of the water collected by plants is below the canopy drip and not at the plant's base and trunk.

Know, when air temperatures are less than noon, the optimal time for water in the morning or evening is to reduce evaporation. Do not dump leaves in the evening as it will promote the production of fungi or mildew, making plants toxic and compromising their health.

It is just as important to know how much water to add as irrigation. Plants should be provided enough water to water the soil at the appropriate rooting depth in the entire plant root region.

This can be measured with a point metal rod called a soil sensor in order to measure the depth of the mud. Just after irrigation, inject the test into the field. The rod glides effortlessly over the watery surface, and it is hard to move until it hits dry land. If it has been decided how long the soil needs to be fully soaked, any time you wash, you will run the wash for the same period of time.

Foot-and-mouth irrigation fosters a shallow root system, and unhealthy plant and water loss. Studies suggest the rooting depths of approximately 12 inches a year, crops and lawns for the following plants; 12-24 inches for perennials and shrubs; and 28-36inches for trees.

Water can only be added as easily as the soil can absorb. O rapidly absorption of water induces flooding, wasting water, and cements the surface of the earth.

Soil should be allowed to dry slightly between watering to provide the oxygen they require with the plant roots. Using the soil sensor every couple of days to test the soil before the device penetrates 4-6 inches deeper in the soil. Three to four inches of mulch keep soils cool, reduces water loss by evaporation, and impedes weed development, which competes for water in the plant.

In hot, dry spring and summer, plants need more water, and varied environmental patterns can influence the amount of water that other plants require. Dry winds also boost the need for water for a farm. During the monsoon, high moisture and rain decrease irrigation requirements. Wherever you stay or what the conditions you have to deal with make sure the plants get ample water and change the watering schedule accordingly.

Young plants and fresh plants should be watered more regularly than older plants. Water should be added in the drip line and above as the roots grow. After they have been developed, they cause plants to dry between watering in one or two years. The plants are adapted to stress and are more tolerant of drought. Efficient irrigation and cooking plants, in general, do not require watering more than once every two to four weeks.

This is because fast-growing plants require more water than slow-growing plants. Many plants are adapted to dry, arid conditions in the desert. These plants have small leaves, gray leaves, and photosynthesizing trunks and leathery or floured leaves or other features that allow them to survive on less water. These plants need considerably less water than species with large dark green leaves, which are less well suited.

Sandy soils absorb water faster and drain quicker than other soil types. Water should be spread more easily and more regularly. Clay soils absorb water gradually and hold water more quickly, allowing water to be added progressively and less often. Water added so rapidly to clay soils is lost, and the damage is induced when it runs out. When a berm has been installed around a plant's root zone to retain soil, soil can be easily added without fear of runoff.

Your garden must be watered properly. Note the four 'Golden Laws' of irrigation when irrigating or watering your garden: 1) know where to drink, 2) know how often drink is to be needed, 3) know how quickly you need it; 4) know how much there is water. Wetter, surface and plant nature impact irrigation laws

Ways to Conserve Water in Your Garden

It is well known that the intake of residential water rises by 10 to 50% during the summer months, and thirsty plants do require water.

Do your water bills reach new heights every summer since your garden washed up? Or, as an environmentally conscious citizen, does it bother you to see a lot of water wasting in your garden? If you answered these questions affirmatively, find some easy methods you may not have considered to maintain your garden water while improving the wellbeing of your plants as a whole.

When to save water during the hour? Mornings and afternoons are good times for watering your lawn. In addition to the major impacts on how well the plants are grown, watering them before growing temperatures decreases evaporation and loss of water. In reality, if you water your plants early in the morning, they will handle the heat of the day better. The watering evening is not recommended because night temperatures are not suitable for the absorption of moisture. But, if because of the lack of moisture, you see your plants wilting or rotting, don't wait for the next morning to water them.

Harvest and reuse of water-Water supplies should not be relegated to boring wells and pipes. Build a water tank to catch rainwater from the Roof Rivers and store the water for your garden. There is no space for you to set up a tiny water tank, so rainwater will potentially help the plants grow even further.

Don't underestimate your cooking water's potential. If you are accustomed to tapping water from boiled or steamed vegetables in the kitchen, it is time to break the habit. Pour this water into a bowl and use it for watering your plants when cooled. In addition to supplying heat, the cooking water provides nutrients that will allow the plants to grow.

If you have a fish tank, use the old water instead of rinsing it down the drain for your plants. The ancient fish tank water is high in nitrogen and phosphorus and will have an incredible effect on your plant health.

Developing a mini compost system is a perfect way to save your garden's soil. Compost preserves and retains nutrients in soil moisture. It eliminates the need to water the plants regularly, including in dry summer months. It is easy to make compost bin-all you need is an old waste bin and biodegradable nitrogen-rich waste. Seal and put the bucket in the sunshine and roll it sometimes.

The Bokashi Bin, which transforms fermented grain and food scrap into nutrient-rich compost, has become a common version of compost bins. Just a few buckets, you can make your own Bokashi Bin-a bucket needs to match just holes in its middle, which are then put within the second bucket. The liquid from fermentation waste will spill into the bottom bucket as the compost matures. The waste is distilled and conserves moisture, while the fermented material is a fertilizer.

Your plant container counts – the size of containers that you use for your plants have a great deal to do with what you use to water them. Many fabrics quickly lose moisture since they are brittle, and you can need to reconsider them. There is certainly no problem with metal pots as they heat up easily and allow the soil to dry up much faster. Do use a less potful, like glazed terracotta containers that are sufficiently porous to keep your plants safe and maintain moisture.

Using Mulch – did you know that mulching will conserve up to 70% of soil water? Some of the best moisture conservation techniques that you can add are a defensive mulch coating on top of your ground. Mulch inhibits the growth of water-consuming plants, avoids the evaporation of water, and also contributes important nutrients to the soil. Of note, mulches will be one of your garden's best water-saving strategies. When picking sets, do tend to be dirty rather than lighter, water-repellent mulches. Coarser mulches remove precipitation to prevent evaporation into the soil. The perfect depth for mulches in a garden bed about 8 centimeters and in a pot about 3 centimeters.

Check the Plants – Certain plants save water practically, and they do not suck dry air. Some of these plants are smaller, especially those with smaller leaves. Also fantastic are fast-growing plants or plants with silver or gray leaves. The thick, leathery, and fuzzy leavened plants require less moisture not to be forgotten.

On the other side, thirsty plants flood with water and will waste energy, time, and resources a lot. Some of these plants are with bigger leaves, fast-growing plants, and plants, which you need to, fertilize a lot. The growing a plant leaves, the greater is the water demand due to transpiration. Develop in smaller plants with minimum water requirements.

Environment and Soils Go Hand in Hand-Have you just had a shower of rain in front of the situation, where you sprayed your plants? Ok, check the weather report periodically for rainfall predictions, and the automatic sprinkler can be turned down. Understand the climate of the area you live in and the seasons.

Windy, dry summers where humidity is less, you need more water for your plants, while higher rainfall, cooler temperatures, and shade decrease the need to water your plants. Although you have no power over weather and seasons, a wise way of retaining water is to provide a couple of garden structures or big plants with a fair amount of shade. In contrast with sandy bare soils, a cooler garden combined with mulched clay soils will save plenty of water.

Get a Humidity Meter-Invest in a Moisture Meter if you just want to learn how much water your plants require to stop overwatering them. This is a low-cost, easy-to-use tool that helps you to read the moisture content of your soil and lets clearly you realize how much more you need to drink.

Unless the moisture meter is 80-100%, it means the soil is too damp, and you should stop watering it completely. If the readings vary from 40 to 70%, the soil is fine, and you don't need to do something about it. On the other hand, a 10-30% reading reveals that the soil is too dry and watered. Having a water meter will let you realize how much water you need, which does not waste or drown your plants.

Using a screwdriver to check the soil moisture if you do not want to invest in a water meter. When the sprinkler falls into the ground quickly, you don't need to spray it. However, it's time to water immediately whether you have to work to get it in or if it fails to get in.

Chapter 7
Pest Control

Insects are always present in our garden. Many times we think that all can harm our plants, but that is not true. Learn about the most common pest insects in the garden, their characteristics and what you can do to control them.

Aphids

Aphids are a tiny fly, measuring 0.9-3 mm. There are over 4,000 species, but some 250 are considered pests. Its color may be gray, white, red or black, and there are wings in some species. Its mouth apparatus is a sucker, meaning it feeds on the plant's sap. We can find plenty of vegetables, like lettuce, tomato, eggplant, cauliflower, spinach, chili, kale, etc. Aphids transmit diseases, so monitoring our plants is very important. We can find them at the leaves and growth points on the underside.

1 Red Aphid

To cool them we can add water on the underside of the plants with biodegradable soap, do it really early in the morning or in the afternoon when the sun does not touch the plants anymore. Some natural enemies of aphids are parasitic wasps (Aphelinus abdominals, Aphidius colemani, Aphidius ervi), Catarina (Coccinellidae), lacewing (Chrysoperla carnea), parasitic fly (Apidoletes sp)

Larvae or caterpillars

There are various forms of larvae in our garden; various sizes and colors. But what exactly is a larva? Larvae are the juvenile stage of some metamorphosis-bearing insects. The larvae which affect our plants come from butterflies or moths of the night.

2 - Larvae or caterpillar

The larvae can be 1-7 cm in size and can have a black, white, gray, brown color. The larvae are insect chewing and can be located on the underside of the leaves, at the point of growth or in the dirt. They attack most plants in our garden, in this botanical family, in particular broccoli, cauliflower, kale and other plants.

To control them, we can use soap and garlic and chili extract with biodegradable water. Apply very early in the morning or evening when the plants no longer receive the rays of the sun. It's a simple method even to extract them by hand. Some natural larvae enemies are lacewing (Chrysoperla carnea) and the Bt (Bacillus thuringiensis) bacteria.

Whitefly

3 - Whitefly

The whitefly is a small (1mm) powdery white insect. This fly feeds on the sap of the plant, reducing its productivity. A side effect of whitefly is disease transmission. We find it on the underside of the leaves of many plants such as; tomatoes, aubergines, pumpkin, cucumber, flowers such as poinsettia and jamaica, among others. Some natural enemies are the Catarina, lacewing, predatory beetles (Orius sp), parasitic wasps (Encarsia sp). We can also apply soapy water or yellow traps.

Leaf miners

4 - Leaf miners

The leaf miner is a small larva that we can find in the leaves of our plants. They make small galleries or paths between the leaves, taking away space for the plant to carry out its photosynthesis. The most effective control is to locate the larva on the leaf and crush it with our fingers, making sure that you do not hurt the plant.

Chapulines

The chapulines are a common pest that can cause a lot of damage since they eat the leaves and, in some cases, the whole plant. These insects can eat any plant. The grasshoppers can be up to 8cm long. For the control of grasshoppers, we can count on spiders, mantises, Bacillus thuringiensis (Bt, bacteria) and Beauveria bassiana (fungus).

Red spider

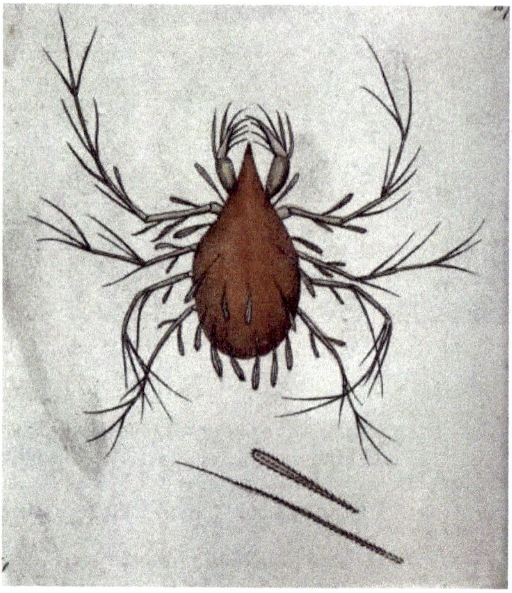

5 - Red Spider

The red spider is a very small insect (0.5mm) that feeds on the sap of plants. Always in a group. These insects form a white spider web on the leaves and stems, thereby protecting themselves from predators. They can attack strawberry, eggplant, squash, tomato, corn, chili, melon, potato, and trees. For its control, an extract of garlic and chili can be applied. If the plant is severely affected, it is best to remove it to avoid spreading to other plants. Good prevention is crop rotation.

Trips

Thrips are small insects that measure between 1-3mm. It is a yellowish-brown or brown color. They feed on the sap of the plant, and they can cause leaf spots and transmit diseases. These insects are attracted to the blue color, and you can put a blue container with water and some soap or sticky traps. Thrips have several natural predators, such as some varieties of mites and the Orius bug (Orius sp).

Mealybugs

Mealybugs are small (6mm) black or grayish in color. Very common behavior in mealybugs is that they curl up to protect themselves, forming a small ball. If our soil is well nourished, it will not be a problem for our garden.

Snails and slugs

Snails and slugs are mollusks that live in humid areas and water reservoirs. They feed on all kinds of plants and can end up destroying the entire garden. We can identify the damage by the traces of mucus that they leave behind. We can prevent the arrival of snails by having our plants in elevated places and using aromatic herbs. Remember they are looking for cool and humid places. For its control, we can use coffee beans, beer traps or eggshells.

Nematodes

Nematodes are small plant parasites found in the soil. Its shape is like an earthworm, and they measure between 0.2-1mm depending on the species. These small individuals feed on the roots of the plants, but there are species that are beneficial (they are biological control for some insects). To control the nematodes in the soil, we can plant garlic cloves, and this will serve as a repellent. It is also important to have a crop rotation and fertilize our soil.

You can find many pests in your garden, but controlling them is not that difficult. Remember to check your garden frequently, once or twice a week. Look well under the leaves, and there you can find many pests and other insects.

Vegetable Gardening Problems – Prevention

There are many alternatives to synthetic insecticides to control some unwanted insects that we commonly call as garden pests. It is first important to know which insects are harmful to plants and which are beneficial, the natural allies of the garden. These allies are very important in preventing pests and diseases as they help to protect the plants against some hungry insects that appear more frequently in the spring. There are still other good practices that must be considered in pest prevention!

How to prevent pests in an organic garden

1. Choose the vegetable varieties most resistant to insects and diseases. Whenever possible, we should choose seeds from organic or biodynamic agriculture. In addition, it is preferable to produce seedlings for transplanting.

2. Provide shelter for natural enemies of pests, such as predatory insects (spiders, ladybugs), bats, and birds.

3. Improve the soil structure, adding organic compost or making green manure. As a result, healthy soil will allow healthier plants to grow.

4. Grow aromatic and medicinal herbs to bring beneficial insects to the garden. In addition, some have a repellent effect on pests.

5. Try to plant in a small space in order to see if there is damage caused by any present pest. In this way, we understand if there is already a pest installed, and should apply home remedies to control.

6. Cut the first infected plants and remove them from the site. So, by removing the residues from the infected crops, we will help to interrupt the insect's biological cycles.

7. Take into account the practices of favorable intercropping of cultures. Consequently, this practice also helps to benefit from more effective management of soil space and nutrients.

8. Always use natural preventive methods, such as biological control. Furthermore, when they are easily visible, we must collect the pests manually.

9. Avoid monocultures in beds or plots with an area greater than 1 m2. As a result, we promote greater biodiversity, cultivating, for example, some flowering plants such as marigolds, chamomile, and capucinhas, among others.

10. Promote crop rotation. Above all, don't grow the same types of vegetables in the same place every year. We can do a 3-year rotation in 3 sites or a 4-year rotation in 4 plots (more advisable).

Treat a garden against pests

Many pests swarm in gardens and attack all plants, whether vegetables, fruit trees or even ornamental plants. Discover how to treat a garden against pests depending on the species you face.

Treat a garden against mealybug

Scale insects generally proliferate on fruit trees from which they suck the sap, causing sores and proliferation of fungi.

To remove them, the use of solutions based on methylated spirits and black soap is necessary. Softer treatment but just as effective: ladybugs, deadly enemies of cochineal.

Fight against aphids

Aphids also suck the sap from plants, slowing their growth. Vectors of viruses and fungi, they readily settle on roses and fruit trees.

Here again, the ladybug can help get rid of the pest, just like nettle manure and repellents (lavender, thyme, mint ...).

Treat plants against snails and slugs

Snails and slugs appreciate the sap of plants and devour their leaves, bulbs, fruits and roots.

The "ramparts" of ash and wood chips installed around the plantations help to slow down these pests. To remove them, there are chemicals based on iron phosphate.

Protect a garden from mites

Some mites (including the red spider) suck the sap from the trees, resulting in desiccation and discoloration of the leaves.

The first bulwark against mites: humidity. Watering the plants well is, therefore, essential. In the case of invasion, there are acaricides, but one can also use the "services" of their predator, Phytoseiulus persimilis.

Treatment against moths

The larvae of the moth (moth) feed on many plants. Leaves, stems, fruits, buds ... are ingested.

Preventive methods to limit egg-laying are essential here: suppress weeds, hoeing, mulching, watering ... If necessary, we will use a phytosanitary product or the Thuringian bacillus (caterpillar killer bacteria).

Treat fruit worm

The codling moth (fruit worm) is a caterpillar that feeds mainly on the flesh of fruits.

To prevent its appearance, there are pheromone traps that limit its fertilization. If necessary, we will spray bacterospeine (natural insecticide) on the affected tree. One can also enshrine spared fruits and destroy those infected.

.

Chapter 8

Common Mistakes to Avoid

Simply put, you have already learned the right way to plant and care for a raised bed garden. When you learn the right way, you avoid making mistakes by acting on assumption and instead act with knowledge and comprehension.

With that said, it never hurts to be thorough. If you've been paying attention, then hopefully you find yourself nodding along with the understanding of how these common beginner mistakes could easily be avoided. If you don't want to make the rookie actions that cost time, money, and energy, and cause major headaches and stomach pains then you are going to want to pay careful attention to these common mistakes that beginners keep making.

Overwatering Your Plants

This is the last chance there is to reinforce the idea that your plants should be too dry than too wet. While plants need plenty of water, too much water is the deadliest thing of all. It gets into the soil around the roots and prevents them from sucking in oxygen. The roots will blacken and die. They go from having a solid texture almost like a piece of string and instead start to feel slimy and gross. This is all happening under the soil, though, so the first sign that most gardeners see is when the leaves of their plants start to go mushy as they rot from the inside, and if you aren't regularly checking your plants you might not see it until the whole plant has started rotting. If you notice this early on the lowest leaves, you might be able to save the plant by digging it out to remove the rotted roots but more often than not it is already too late.

So the best way to avoid this tragic experience is to avoid overwatering your plants. Always give the finger test before watering and if you are unsure then be cautious and wait a day. It only takes a moment but it can save you the work of removing and replanting your crops. Plants will begin to wilt when they are overly thirsty and this can be a sign to water them. But make sure this wilting isn't just due to the noonday sun. Some plants will wilt in order to protect themselves from the hottest temperatures of the day. Once the sun starts to set, they will stop wilting. Since you should never water your plants at night anyway, check for wilt in the morning to get a more accurate reading. Noonday wilting has tricked many beginners into a panicked watering in the afternoon and this leaves water in the soil overnight. Even if your plants appear to be dehydrated, wait until the morning to water them. It may feel odd but it is the healthier option.

Skipping Out on Maintenance

Maintenance is another one of those mistakes that happen often enough to be embarrassing. There is simply no excuse for leaving your garden completely untended to. When you do this, you are choosing to completely ignore any signs of danger that you might have been able to catch early. If you left your house for a vacation, you would lock the front door. When you stop maintaining your raised garden beds, you are leaving them with their door wide open for pests, weeds, critters, and disease.

The biggest problems with untended beds are weeds and dead plant matter. Weeds will completely take over a raised garden bed if you don't catch them early. Skipping out on maintenance for half a week could lead to an infestation you are unable to beat without replacing the soil. Weeds that get out of hand will starve out your plants and this will lead to far more leaves dropping off them than normal. This increases the amount of dead plant matter in the garden bed and offers more space for pests and diseases to get an entry hold. Both weeds and dead plant matter are issues on their own but when maintenance is left ignored, they end up being a one-two punch to your raised garden bed and the health of your plants.

Ignoring the Drainage

When you mix up your soil, you are doing it to create a quickly draining texture. Raised garden beds drain better due to their elevated positions but you still need to use well-draining soil. Introducing too many plants will block up the soil and slow down the draining, while preventing anyone plant from getting enough nutrients. Weeds will also slow down the drainage. But the biggest problem is failing to include drainage holes in the raised bed frame itself. Depending on the material used, water will have an easier or harder time getting out even with a drainage hole. You need to balance this all when building and mixing soil. Many beginners only take into account their soil or their drainage holes and not the whole spectrum of influence.

Using the Wrong Soil

We mixed a general-purpose garden soil mixture. This mixture will work for many plants but not for all of them. You need to do your research on what you are going to grow to see if this soil mixture will work for them. Typically, most of what you want to grow is either going to enjoy this or it will want something with a little more of a sandy texture. More minerals in the soil will increase the speed of drainage but not every plant enjoys a sandy soil.

The disappointing thing with using the wrong soil is that you may not realize it is wrong when you first start using it because it does a decent enough job. You might think that your plants are doing fine when they are smaller than they should be. But when you provide them with the right soil, you will notice a major difference in the size and depth of color they take. This is especially true if the soil you have chosen doesn't have enough nutrients in it.

But the other issue with soil is that the right soil last year might not be the right soil a year later. The quality of soil degrades over time, more so if it is reliant on organic components like compost. It is important to pay close attention to your soil. Degrading soil will start to drain much slower. You may need to mix in some more minerals and compost but this can be hard to do after you have planted your raised beds for the year. A good way to get a heads up on this issue is to water your beds before you plant anything. Doing this will let you see if they are draining properly or not. Take a few minutes also to see if it "feels" right. If you have been using the same soil mixture for some time then you will have a sense of how it is supposed to feel. If it feels off then it will be time to amend it to make sure it still works as intended.

Chapter 9
Tips and Tricks for Growing Healthy Plants

A fair bit of finding your green thumb is trial and error. What works for one gardener may not necessarily prove to be effective for another. However, there is a lot to be said for taking in all of the advice and learning what does work for others. That said, here are some of my very own secrets to the gardening success that I enjoy.

Sticking to Favorite Varieties.

There are almost endless options to try in terms of vegetable varieties. It's a great idea to try something new each and every year. But as you gain your gardening confidence, and learn more about how to utilize your available space best, you may just find that you are sticking to a few favorites. Here are some of my favorite varieties and some must-haves for all vegetable gardens.

Tomatoes. Tomatoes come in all shapes, sizes, colors, and even flavors. For large slicers you simply cannot go wrong with Brandywine. A pink beefsteak, this tomato can reach almost 2lbs per fruit. With bold flavors and an interesting texture, this is a must-have for your garden. It's also found in black, yellow and red varieties, but gardeners tend to agree that the original pink offers the most flavor.

Cherry tomatoes are also popular, and you simply can't go wrong with Sweet 100. Sun Sugar is another tasty variety. Consider also looking for white cherry tomatoes. They taste almost like a dessert fruit when chilled for a few hours. If tomato sauce is on your agenda this year, then you'll have plenty of success with Roma tomatoes.

Peas. Easy to grow and incredibly sweet right out of the pod, peas are a spring must-have. Sugar Pod snap peas are a tasty option that you'll enjoy in stir fries, stews, or just raw right off of the vine. Mr. Big is a variety that produces plump peas, and it's a great fun choice for kids to grow. For the best in sweetness, Garden Sweet is a prolific and low-maintenance option.

Beans. Falling under the category of being low-maintenance, there are endless options for beans. Some of my favorite pole beans are Kentucky Blue, Monte Gusto (a tasty yellow wax bean), and Purple King. These three should produce well through summer and up to the first frosts. Bush bean favorites are French Stringless, and Italian Rose. With so many options for beans, you should definitely experiment until you find your favorites. Beans are also great for crop rotation as they help to replenish nutrients in the soil for other crops.

Summer squash. Most zucchini and yellow summer squash are prolific and low-maintenance options. But I do like to mix things up a little bit by adding some Green Tiger zucchini, and of course a variety of Patty Pans. The Sunburst Patty Pans offer a rich flavor that you'll quickly find yourself addicted to. Verte et Blanc squash are very similar to

Patty Pans, but they are so pretty to grow; and of course are incredibly tasty.

Winter squash. No garden is complete with growing butternut. Waltham and Butterbush will deliver big. You'll get plenty of squash, with each boasting a rich buttery taste that you will never find in store-bought squash. Buttercup and Lakota winter squash are also tasty, easy options to grow. Any true Hubbard squash will also give you plenty of squash for those pumpkin pies when the holiday season rolls around. A little known secret is that many pumpkin pies are actually made with Hubbard squash!

Potatoes. Spuds can be enjoyed at any size, so feel free to harvest them at any time. But if you are looking for large potatoes then you simply cannot go wrong with Yukon Gold. The Rio Grande Russet is also a great reliable option. If you're looking for something a little bit different, try growing purple or blue potatoes. The All Blue or Purple Majesty varieties are delicious and hold their color when cooked. Purple mashed potatoes can be a lot of fun for the whole family.

Onions. No winter garden should be without onions. Red Candy is a large and sweet red onion that you'll find easy to grow; for a sweet yellow onion you'll appreciate Walla Walla Sweet. Onions can be one of those subjective flavors, so try a couple of different varieties until you find the ones that best suit your taste buds.

Start with the offerings at your local garden center, and you'll soon find what does and doesn't work for you.

Rain Barrels

Water is certainly easy to gain access to, but one thing I have found not just to be a huge time saver, but also a huge money saver, is to invest in rain barrels. Rain barrels collect and store rainwater that would otherwise be lost as it pours from your roof and other surfaces.

Typically rain barrels are 55 gallon drums, PVC couplings, a vinyl hose, and a screen to keep it free from debris. Relatively easy and budget-friendly to construct, your rain barrels can sit underneath any gutter downspout around your home.

During the summer months your garden is going to need extra water. Watering your vegetables could boost your water bill a fair bit. But during dry periods, having your rain barrel to rely on could make quite a positive difference. Whether you purchase a kit or build one of your own designs, you'll find that rain barrels are an incredible addition to your garden.

Raised Bed Materials

There are so many options for building raised beds. I started out with kits using plastic molded frames, and now I've moved on to a design of my own. I've tried out most of the different materials in my pursuit of raised bed perfection. My favorite is pressure treated lumber. It's affordable, durable, and easy to work with. With pressure treated lumber, I can build beds of any size and height to suit my needs exactly. Bricks and cinderblocks also work well.

Garden Twine

To make sure that you always have garden twine on hand when it is needed, simply stick a ball of twine inside of a clay pot. Pull the end of the twine through the drainage hole and set the pot upside down in a convenient location. This way you'll never have to go on the hunt for twine to secure your tomatoes or squash. Those same small clay pots can make great cloches for your tender young plants in the event of an unexpected frost.

Feeding Your Plants

Fertilizers and compost certainly do the job, but there are some little tricks that can give your plants a boost. When you next steam or boil vegetables, don't pour the water out. Allow it to cool and then pour it over your garden. You will be impressed at how well your plants respond to this little nutrient boost. Leftover coffee grounds and tea leaves can add a bit of an acid boost for plants that love acidic soil. Rooibos tea is one of the many great tea options you should consider.

Chapter 10
Herbs to Grow

A raised bed can provide the perfect setting to build an herb garden. It can be put wherever it serves you and can be easily maintained.

Siting

If you are preparing to use the herbs to prepare, it is better to position your elevated bed comfortably near the kitchen. Venturing into the garden on a quiet, rainy, wintery evening to hunt for rosemary for your roast lamb can be irritating. Choose a dry, sunny place with no frost pockets, bearing in mind that some Mediterranean herbs can enjoy full sunlight during the season.

Soil

General mixed compost with favorable pH is suitable for growing herbs. Try to avoid high nitrogen feeds and improvers because they encourage rapid growth at the cost of the delicate taste of the plant. Herbs prefer soil well-drained and make sure they contain plenty of organic matter.

Layout

Grow the larger plants in the middle of the bed like rosemary, and the shorter growing herbs near the edges. This equally distributes shade and helps you to stretch across the bed to plant and reap. You are leaving space between them when planting your herbs to allow for development and spread.

Care

Secure small, young clove-like herbs until they are formed. Take time to weed around the plants and remove dead limbs and leaves. This can be accomplished quite easily with uplifted bed access. Using the manufacturer's directions, feed the plants regularly with a general-purpose fertilizer. Deadhead flowers can funnel energy and development into the foliage as they begin to fade. Many herbs can last just one season, though others will go on year after year. Take the opportunity to stock up by taking cuttings or splitting the farm.

Harvesting

Most plants can benefit from continued harvesting because foliage development is encouraged by cutting herbs while you are taking cuttings. Don't slash the plant by more than a third, and always snip just above the closest intersection of the root. The cut herbs can be used directly in the oven, or processed for frozen or dried later. For a savory salad dressing, you can also catch the delicious flavor of your freshly picked herbs flavored with butter.

What to Grow?

In most allotment plots, growing the crops you like is good. This is mostly the case for herbs, although it is necessary to plant other varieties just to provide a good ornamental aromatic show. Elevated beds will give you the room to grow a wide selection of tasty culinary herbs whilst offering a splendid variegated view. Examples commonly found include Basil, Rosemary, Parsley, Chives, Tarragon, Garlic, Oregano, and Thyme.

Mint: A beautiful and so flexible crop of containers. It can be used for anything from tea and mojitos to mint and chutney coriander. It's also easy to grow – it'll even cope with demanding sunny spaces that just get a little light. However, it is a selfish beast, which needs regular feeding in order to grow well. Place each plant in its own 5-liter jar, keep it watered well and pick it up daily. Once your plant is grown, each spring after its winter dies back, take it out of the pot and split it into halves or thirds, and report it with fresh compost. This helps keep the vigor – and offers you knew plants to enhance or give away your mint range.

Chives: Excellent in salads snipped over soups or applied to many tables as a garnish. In the season, the flowers are bright, taste yummy- and the bees do enjoy them. This is another simple one to develop and requires just four or five hours of sunshine. Make sure it doesn't dry out because wet soil is like chives.

Sage/Bay/Thyme/Rosemary: These traditional herbs are easy to grow with unique flavors and are good for soups, stocks, meats, pasta, and more. They do not like damp roots – but they thrive in well-drained soil and do not overwater. You may develop sage from seed; the others are best purchased as plants or grown from cuttings (bay from cuttings is difficult though).

Parsley: This is sluggish to get out of the seed, but once it's grown, it will send you leave for almost two years before it flowers and dies.

Coriander: In the beginning, coriander planted flowers easily and goes to work. You may try to postpone this (maintaining it well watered and fed, increasing it in a shadier place, and cutting the leaves regularly), but inevitably, whatever you do, will happen. Don't worry: the flowers are attractions for hoverflies (whose larvae consume aphids), and they are tasty green seeds. Throughout the late autumn, you will get buds, the plants will withstand most winters, and in the spring it will grow strong and green again. Basil: What the air needs. It is best grown in a dry, light, protected location (it thrives in greenhouses) and sown in June when the weather warms. Even it doesn't like going to bed with the damp roots-so rise in the morning in well-drained soil and water. Sorrel: It has a solid, sour flavor and a bit of lemony. Fried, sorrel shapes traditional egg and salmon combos, or you can chop up a few fresh leaves and apply them to salads. Growing in a jar is facile. Grow six to eight plants (easy to start from seed) in a window box with at least four hours of sunshine, and it will give you a hit of flavor throughout the year. Select the leaves outside, and it will continue to produce new leaves. As long as you remember two rules, you can grow herbs together in pots: Consider combining plants (such as chives, spinach, and coriander) with plant-like soils (such as rosemary, thyme, garlic, bay, and Oregano). And select similar size herbs for the same pot-for example, large rosemary will swamp a small thyme plant. So search for a thin, portable type of rosemary if you want to blend rosemary and thyme with it.

Chapter 11

Flowers That Flourish in Raised Beds

Making use of raised garden beds for the cultivation of flowers may not appeal to everyone. After all, how many flowers can you actually eat?

Having said that, however, the joy and interest that beautiful blooms bring to every garden cannot be denied.

Flowers also attract a variety of pollinators, among which is the much-maligned and seriously jeopardized honey bee.

Tara Nolan (2017), in her article, Tips for Planting and Making Raised Flower Beds, agrees that growing blooms alongside vegetables, herbs, and fruits have many advantages.

Careful planning of your raised bed floral garden can give rise to many hours of pleasure as well as plenty of bouquets of summer flowers to brighten your home and cheer neighbors and friends.

When planting from seeds, ensure you carefully note the requirements for each variety as well as their height at maturity. Taller plants should be placed towards the center of the raised bed, allowing easier access to the shorter flowers that you can plant around the edges.

Feeding your floral garden with good nutrients and keeping it well hydrated is of the utmost importance. Mulching will keep the roots protected and ensure these do not dry out too quickly in warmer weather.

Nolan (2017) suggests sunflowers, zinnias, daylilies, and cosmos are easy to grow and produce an attractive show. Gladiolus and lilies may be successfully planted where there are no squirrels to decimate the bulbs.

Important Aspects to Consider When Choosing Flowers

According to her article, 21 Easiest Flowers for Beginners, Linda Hagen (2019) suggests the following important points should be carefully considered as you set out to plan your new raised bed garden.

Take Careful Note of Your Garden Area

Consider the amount of available space you have for your raised garden beds. Get acquainted with the gardening site.

Take the position of the planned garden into consideration as well as whether there will be sufficient sunlight for your plants.

Check the type of soil in your area as well as its ability to hold water. Good soil quality will ensure healthy plant growth.

Know your frost cycle, and ensure you plant crops and flowers according to what will grow best in your zone.

Take a good look at the plants growing in your neighborhood. This will give you a good idea of what is likely to grow successfully in your new garden.

Choose Flowers to Suit Your Style

The same article suggests that although gardening can be a wonderfully therapeutic experience, beginners should remember to curb their enthusiasm for overindulging in too many colors and varieties of blooms. It is prudent to start off deciding on a basic color scheme that will suit your personality and style.

If you prefer a garden that whispers tranquility and peace, choose flowers in shades of blue, purple, and soft pinks with a dash of white and yellow.

However, if your style leans to the more vibrant and exciting side, a mix of cheerful, brightly colored flowers may suit you better.

The recommendation in the same article by Garden Design Magazine (2019b) is to avoid too much variety and colors that clash as this is likely to affect the overall beauty of your garden adversely.

Inventive Designs Catch the Imagination

Think fragrance, movement, color, and the overall final impact you would like your raised bed garden to have.

Piet Oudolf, the internationally renowned garden designer from the Netherlands, designs his gardens around the structure and shapes of the flowers he plants (Garden Design Magazine, 2019b). Piet suggests choosing blooms that have solid, stout's stalks so that after they flower, these stems, topped by their attractive seed pods, will make an attractive display when covered with snow.

Perennials come in a variety of shapes that include bells, spikes, plumes, screens, and buttons to name but a few.

Careful consideration of and inventive grouping of a variety of plant shapes will lead to pockets of interest and surprise in your new garden.

Plan on layering your flowers so they blend together as naturally as possible to create a free-flowing bank of gorgeous blooms.

Depending on the position of your raised bed garden, consider placing taller plants towards the center or back with plants of medium height next. The shorter, bushier plants should be placed towards the front and sides of the garden. You can add objects such as a statue or a boulder or perhaps a birdbath to your raised bed garden. These items will create added interest and will encourage birds that are useful pollinators into this eco-friendly space. Consider planting lots of foliage-producing plants as well if you intend to cultivate flowers for cutting (Garden Design Magazine, 2019b).

Fair Flowers for Floral Fragrance

Choosing flowers for your raised bed may be quite an overwhelming experience to begin with. There are many different varieties available, each with specific characteristics of its own.

Some flowers are prized for their astonishingly beautiful colors, hues, and shades while others are chosen for their tall, majestic stems. Then there are those gorgeous blooms that enthrall us with their enchanting fragrance.

Other flowers are valued for their medicinal properties and others find favor in being the most suitable for bordering your raised beds in cheerful abundance.

In her article, 21 Easiest Flowers for Beginners, Hagen (2019) suggests a wide variety of easy-to-grow flowers for any beginner gardener to enjoy. Among these, she includes the following suitable annuals that will be suitable for raised garden beds:

Dianthus

ZONE: 3-9

These showy, fragrant flowers surrounded by lush, evergreen foliage bloom from May to August and grow to a height of about 20 inches.

They flourish in well-drained soil and require small amounts of water, preferring not to become water-logged.

Dianthus grows well in either full sun or semi-shade. These small, colorful flowers are resistant to deer and will bring gorgeous splashes of color to your raised bed garden.

Fuchsias

ZONE: Annual, everywhere except for 10-11

The Fuchsias' gorgeous shades of pink, magenta, purple, lavender, and white make for attractive displays, ideal for hanging baskets on patios or in trees where they thrive in shady spots.

These lovely plants prefer moist, well-drained soil and require regular pruning to attract new growth. They attract hummingbirds, bees, and butterflies.

Fuchsias grown in Southern California and Bay Areas are prone to fuchsia mites.

Geraniums

ZONE: 10-11 (Grown as an annual everywhere else)

These hardy, sun-loving plants that enjoy rich, well-drained soil are ideal for raised bed gardens.

Geraniums come in a variety of shades from magenta through red, pink, lavender, and white.

These plants can reach heights of 24 inches when mature. They attract birds, bees, and butterflies.

Lupines

ZONE: 4-8 where they are often grown as an annual

Lupines are tall, quite majestic plants that can reach a height of four feet.

These happy, little flowers enjoy being in the full sun in cooler climates and in partial shade in warmer areas. They are attractive to butterflies.

Lupins come in a variety of gorgeous blues, lavenders, and pinks. There are white and yellow varieties as well. They grow well from seed and are good self-sowers.

These plants require a good, deep soaking but their roots must be allowed to dry out between watering.

Morning Glories

ZONE: Annual

Morning glories love the full sun and bloom late summer or early in the fall. These climbers in shades of blue, purple, white, and pink make excellent plants for trellis covers and readily self-sow.

Although these plants attract butterflies as well as birds, the seeds are highly poisonous if eaten.

Morning glories prefer fertilized, well-drained soil and require regular watering during dry periods.

Pansies

ZONE: 6-10 grown as perennials/biennials

Pansies are ideal plants for warmer areas where they will bloom throughout the winter and well into early spring.

The plants prefer well-fertilized, well-drained soils and require regular watering. They enjoy sunny conditions but will also thrive in partial shade.

Pansies come in a variety of attractive colors and grow to a maximum height of nine inches.

Snapdragon

ZONE: Annuals everywhere except for 5-10 where they grow as perennials

These attractive 6-15 inch tall plants come in a variety of lovely colors from white, pink, and lavender to red, orange, and peach.

Snapdragons will enjoy a sunny spot in your garden and will bloom from spring through fall. These interestingly-shaped flowers attract butterflies.

They require well-drained, rich soil and regular watering.

Sunflowers

ZONE: Annual

These cheerful, yellow flowers grow to a height of between 3 and 16 feet. Because of their height and their brittle stems, to ensure your sunflowers remain upright, it is prudent to place supports into the ground for these plants.

They are tough plants that cope well in most soil types and are drought resistant, so they require less water than other plants.

Sunflowers do best in full sun and bloom during the summer. They attract bees, butterflies, and some seed-eating birds.

Sunflowers make a great backdrop in a garden or as a cut flower.

Sweet Peas

ZONE: Annual

These wonderfully scented plants come in a variety of colors and make an attractive addition to any garden.

They prefer regular watering in good-quality loamy soil that is well-drained.

Sweet peas do well in full sun and can be successfully grown on a trellis as their soft stems require added support.

Zinnias

ZONE: Annual

These summer bloomers that grow well in full sunlight come in a variety of shades of red, orange, yellow, white, and some pinks.

Although zinnias are fairly hardy plants, they prefer richer soil that drains well. Their water requirements are minimal.

Zinnias bloom during the summer and can reach a height of about 24 inches. They are, therefore, suitable flowers for cutting as their long, sturdy stems look good in a vase.

Helpful Flowers Medicinal or Edible Purposes

Important Advice on Edible Flowers

Perhaps the most important advice you can receive about edible flowers is as follows:

- Eat only confirmed edible varieties and preferably those that are organically grown.
- Avoid eating flowers grown by retailers as these are often sprayed with pesticides.
- thoroughly wash the flowers before consuming them.
- Make sure to eat only those areas of the flower that are recommended. In most instances, it is usually only the petals that are edible.

- IF IN DOUBT, DO NOT EAT!

Advice on Flowers for Medicinal Purposes

Many plants and flowers are well-known for their medicinal and healing qualities. However, once again, be very sure you are working with the correct plant and you understand its specific use.

1. Calendula

These flowers have a tangy, peppery taste and the petals lend a yellow hue to food. The plant is sometimes called "poor man's saffron," says Debbie Wolfe (2019) in her article entitled The Ten Best Edible Flowers to Grow in Your Garden.

Calendula flowers have skin-healing properties, continues Wolfe (2019). Calendula oil can be found in certain ointments used for the treatment of acne, sun protection, and wound healing.

2. Cosmos

These gorgeous long-blooming, sun-loving flowers can reach a height of about 60 inches when they mature.

Their delicate shades of purple, lavender, pink, and white will lend peace and harmony to your garden. When planted close together, cosmos flowers make a wonderfully, attractive display. Cosmos grow quickly from seed in a variety of soil that should be well-drained.

They are useful in repelling mosquitoes.

Cosmos Flowers. (n.d.)

3. Echinacea

Known also as cornflower, the roots and seed head of the echinacea herb have well-known healing qualities that are often used as a remedy for colds.

Besides their medicinal properties, the attractive petals of echinacea can be used to add interesting splashes of color to a dish.

Conclusion

Thank you for making it to the end. Starting a raised bed garden is a great way to accommodate that budding little gardener in your family. It is the ideal way for kids to learn about nature; they will see the wonder of a little seedling emerging from the ground, growing tiny leaves and later develop into a mature plant with fruit. Planting in raised beds will make it convenient for both you and the young ones to reach every plant in the box without ending up with muddy feet or knees full of dirt.

Now that you have all the information needed, it is time to get going. Walk around your available space during the day to find a sunny location. Once you have decided where you want to place your raised bed, decide on the size and dimensions. Make a list of everything you will need, from the soil, compost and other materials, to the frames. Once your bed is up and filled up with the soil mixture, it is time to turn your attention to the plants. Select the type of veggies you want to grow according to the guidelines I have provided. If you want to grow plants from seeds, you will have to do some prior planning since it will take time for them to develop into seedlings ready to be planted outside in your box. Otherwise, you can purchase seedlings to plant directly into your raised beds. Now most of the work is done and the fun part starts. While you wait for your veggies to grow, a little attention is needed; water them regularly and keep your eyes peeled for any pests or weeds. Then wait for the fruit to mature and start harvesting! Growing vegetables in raised beds makes gardening a pleasure. With limited time and space, you can grow an abundance of food in a small area. The benefits are numerous; fewer weeds and pests, better drainage, better soil, no compacting of the soil, less pain potential for you, the gardener, to name but a few. Your friends will envy your neat, attractive garden and harvest of healthy, tasty vegetables. I hope you've realized how easy it is to build a raised garden bed. It doesn't take very much in the way of carpentry skills at all. In fact, it's probably one of the simplest projects you can take on.

And yet, raised garden beds are amongst the most flexible techniques you can use when designing your garden. If you wish, you can certainly build very traditional raised garden beds. But you can also leave tradition behind and build organic or exotic or natural looking raised garden beds. You can build them in wood, in plastic, in stone or in many other materials. In fact, you are only restricted by you access to the materials and by your own imagination.

Raised garden beds provide the experienced gardener with the ability to create micro-environments of soil and moisture. On the other hand, they bring the pleasure of gardening to those with restriction in their ability to perform traditional gardening.

In short, raised garden beds are the epitome of flexibility allowing a gardener to leave the restrictions of their soil and environment behind.

I encourage you to try them for yourself.

CPSIA information can be obtained
at www.ICGtesting.com
Printed in the USA
LVHW081238271020
669935LV00010B/136

9 781801 110914